# AMAZING ANCIENT FACTS AND JOKES

I'm mad about museums!

Special thanks to Toby Battersby for his gorilla joke on page 22

First published 2017 by Nosy Crow Ltd
The Crow's Nest, Baden Place,
Crosby Row, London SE1 1YW

www.nosycrow.com

ISBN 978 0 85763 867 0

Published in collaboration with the British Museum

A CIP catalogue record for this book is available from the British Library.

Printed and bound in the UK by Clays Ltd, St Ives Plc.

Papers used by Nosy Crow are made
from wood grown in sustainable forests.

1 3 5 7 9 8 6 4 2

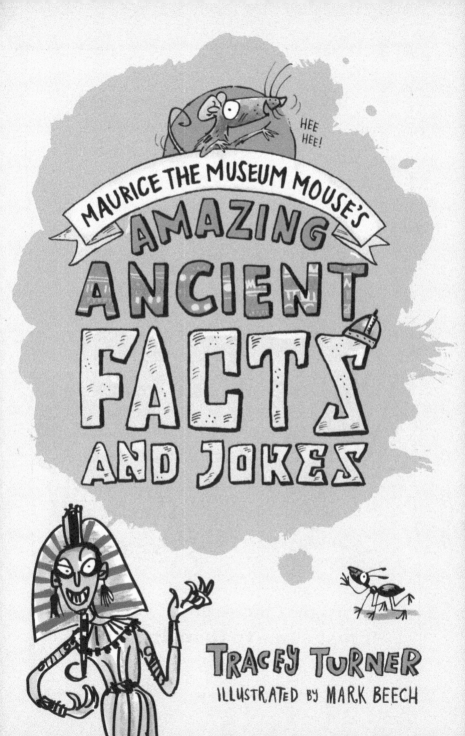

HEE HEE!

# MAURICE THE MUSEUM MOUSE'S AMAZING ANCIENT FACTS AND JOKES

## TRACEY TURNER

### ILLUSTRATED BY MARK BEECH

What did the musically talented
young Egyptian mummies do?
**They formed a boy band-age.**

How did the Chinese invent gunpowder?
**It just came to them in a flash.**

# Foul Fact

Ancient Roman toothpaste and mouthwash contained human wee. Urine imported from Portugal was the most expensive because it was supposed to be the best type of wee for whitening teeth.

# Festering Fact

The ancient Romans also used human wee to do laundry, and left large containers in the street to collect the pee of passers-by.

Urgh, that's disgusting!

Who did the mummy invite
to his party?
**Anyone he could dig up.**

What happened to the Celtic warrior
on his birthday?
**He became a year older.**

Did you hear about the boastful
Egyptian pharaoh?
**She Sphinx she's the best.**

Which barbarian warrior was
always eating?
**Attila the Hungry.**

# Funny Fact

The Vikings had some unflattering nicknames, such as Ragnar Hairy-Breeches, Olaf the Stout, Ulf the Unwashed, Einar Belly-Shaker and Ketill Flatnose.

# Foul Fact

The Aztecs grew crops on floating gardens which were fertilised with human waste.

My favourite book is *Rodent's Revenge*, by Ivor Tail.

THE LIFE OF VLAD III
by Dick Tater

A THOUSAND YEARS OF HISTORY
by Anne O'Domini

A PIRATE'S GUIDE TO PARROTS
by L O Polly

THE SPANISH FLEET
by R Marda

THE WORLD BEFORE CARS
by Orson Cart

THE INVENTION OF SPECTACLES
by Seymour Withem

What's brown and 5,000 miles long?
**The Great Wall-nut of China.**

What do you call a Roman
emperor with a cold?
**Julius Sneezer.**

What do you call an
axe-wielding Visigoth?
**Whatever he tells you to.**

What do you call a Stone Age joke?
**Pre-hysterical.**

# Fascinating Fact

People have been getting tattoos since ancient times. The body of a Stone Age man, preserved in the ice in the Alps, has 61 prehistoric tattoos!

What was Genghis Khan's
favourite circus act?
**He always goes for
the juggler.**

On what date do wars usually start?
**March fourth.**

# Foul Fact

The ancient Romans had
a goddess of sewers, Venus
Cloacina. Her shrine was also the
entrance to Rome's main sewer,
the Cloaca Maxima.

Why are mummies good at
keeping secrets?
**They can keep things under
wraps for centuries.**

I'm a wrap star!

# Pharaoh Fact

Hatshepsut became the first female pharaoh of ancient Egypt. She was often shown wearing the false ceremonial beard that male pharaohs wore, in order to make her look more powerful.

What do you call an ancient ant?
**An antique.**

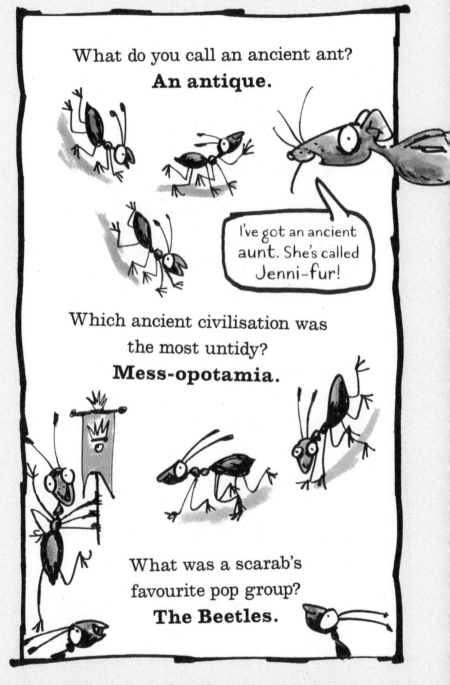

I've got an ancient aunt. She's called Jenni-fur!

Which ancient civilisation was the most untidy?
**Mess-opotamia.**

What was a scarab's favourite pop group?
**The Beetles.**

The Aztec emperor Montezuma was
presented with a treasure trove of
gold and jewels by one of his warriors.
'What treasure!' said Montezuma.
'How did you come by it?'
The warrior replied, 'I've defeated your
enemies to the east, and looted their
villages.' 'But I have no enemies in the
east!' exclaimed Montezuma.
'Well,' said the warrior,
**'you do now.'**

# Pharaoh Fact

There is some speculation about exactly how ancient Egyptian pharaoh Tutankhamun died. His mummy is badly injured down the left side and is missing its heart, which was considered by the Egyptians to be the body's most important part.

Which warring Mongol leader was arrested for fraud?
**Genghis Con.**

# Foul Food Fact

The Spartans of ancient Greece ate black broth, fabled to include boiled pigs' legs, blood and vinegar – it was the Spartan army's staple diet.

Egyptian rulers might have been power-crazed tyrants . . .
**But at least they were pharaoh.**

What's an ancient Greek monster's favourite cheese?
**Gorgon-zola.**

Did someone say cheese?

Which barbarian ape attacked
the Roman Empire?
**Gorilla the Hun.**

The Vikings sometimes
had money-saving sales on
their longships.
**It was quite an oar-deal.**

What do you call a mummified cat?
**A first-aid kit.**

# Flabbergasting Fact

In the 1300s, the Mongol army captured the city of Caffa by catapulting dead bodies infected with plague over the city walls.

What's Medusa's favourite type of cake?
**Rock cakes.**

# Freaky Fact

If a Viking warrior died while far away from home, his friends would boil his body to remove the flesh and take the bones home with them to be buried.

What did the ancient Greeks like eating with their crackers? **Socra-cheese.**

Yum, me too!

What do you call an ancient Briton
who plays a wind instrument?
**An Anglo-Saxophonist.**

What was the capital of Persia?
**P.**

Why did the Mayan throw
the calendar out of the window?
**To see time fly.**

Who was round and purple and
conquered the Persian Empire?
**Alexander the Grape.**

How did ancient Egyptians keep
birds away from their crops?
**With a scarab-crow.**

What did the Roman soldier say
when he ate the mouse?
**Nothing. He was gladiator.**

# Festering Fact

Celtic chieftains were buried with valuable and useful things like jewellery and weapons. Around 2,500 years ago, a German chief was buried with a cauldron containing 400 litres of mead and his nail clippers (among other things).

Nail clippers?!

Who was round and purple and
Empress of Russia?
**Catherine the Grape.**

Heh, heh!

Which hairstyle do Vikings like best?
**Crew cuts.**

\* Did you know that
Vikings didn't actually
wear horned helmets
like this one? That's
just a myth!

# Fascinating Fact

Empress Wu Zetian was the only
woman to become Empress of
China and rule in her own right.
She ruled China during the
Tang Dynasty.

Why did Romans
drink so much wine?
**Just Bacchus.**

# Frightful Fact

The Aztecs believed that the god Tlaloc brought the rain, and in return demanded fresh human hearts as a sacrifice.

Sounds like a tall tail to me.

Which explorer was good at sport played on horseback?

**Marco Polo.**

# Fascinating Fact

The leader of the Incas was
the Sapa Inca, who was supposed
to be descended from the sun god.
He never wore the same clothes
twice and, so as not to be seen
by just anybody, wore a cloth
over his face if he went outside.

# Flabbergasting Fact

In ancient Egypt, people would
shave off their eyebrows as
a sign of grief when a pet cat died.
They'd carry on mourning until
their eyebrows grew back.

That's completely crackers!

Who was the biggest Egyptian
mummy of them all?
**Two-tonne Khamun.**

How was the Roman Empire divided
into the Eastern Roman Empire and
the Western Roman Empire?
**With a pair of Caesars.**

Where did teachers send
sick Viking children?
**To the school
Norse.**

How do mummies relax?
**They unwind a little.**

Which roads are haunted by the
ghosts of Roman soldiers?
**Dead ends.**

# Foul Fact

An ancient Egyptian cure
for toothache involved
applying a dead mouse
to the sore tooth.

Eeeek!
Get me out
of here!

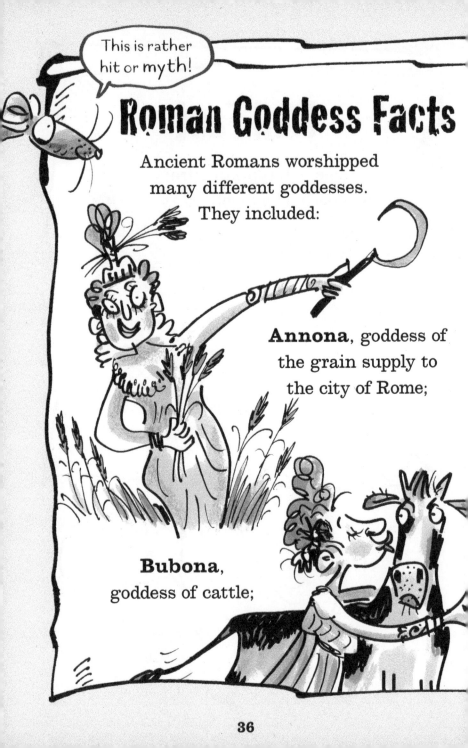

This is rather hit or myth!

# Roman Goddess Facts

Ancient Romans worshipped many different goddesses. They included:

**Annona**, goddess of the grain supply to the city of Rome;

**Bubona**, goddess of cattle;

**Mellona**, goddess of bees;

**Devera**, goddess of the brooms used to purify temples;

**Cardea**, goddess of door hinges.

# Festering Fact

No one knows what really happened to the remains of the prophet John the Baptist, but several churches and a museum claim to have his head, and two different monasteries say they have his right hand.

I'm laughing my head off!

What's the favourite food of Cleopatra's ghost?
**Ghoulash.**

Why did mammoths have
woolly coats?
**Because they would have
looked ridiculous in anoraks.**

Who refereed tennis
matches in ancient Rome?
**The Roman Umpire.**

What has ten heads, twenty feet
and twenty hands?
**Ten mummies.**

Oops! Now it's
only nine heads!

Why were Genghis Khan's
Mongolian warriors so fit?
**They had to keep going up
and down the steppes.**

# Pharaoh Fact

Egyptian pharaoh Khufu's Great
Pyramid became one of the Seven
Wonders of the World, and it was
already ancient in Roman times.
There's plenty of room inside it for
Saint Paul's Cathedral and the
Houses of Parliament.

# Froggy Fact

The ancient Roman writer, Pliny the Elder, wrote about a cure for toothache: catch a frog during a full moon, open the creature's mouth and spit into it, then tell the frog to go away and take your toothache with it. He also suggested using mouse poo as a cure for bad breath.

I wouldn't recommend it!

Why did Hannibal ride elephants
over the Alps?
**They were too heavy to carry.**

Why was Boudicca buried under
King's Cross train station?
**Because she was dead.**

What sort of view do you get
from the top of a pyramid?
**As pharaoh the
eye can see.**

Gulp! It's a
long way down.

Did you hear about the cross-eyed
history teacher?
**She couldn't control
her pupils.**

# Freaky Fact

To cure blindness in ancient Egypt, people mixed a ground-up pig's eye, a type of metal called antimony, red ochre and honey, then poured it into the ear of the blind person.

I doubt that worked very well!

Did you know Archimedes was
fond of food?

**He was always thinking
about pi.**

Did they play tennis in
ancient Babylon?

**Yes, lots of people served
in the royal court.**

# Flabbergasting Fact

Ashurnasirpal II of Assyria described himself in an inscription as a glorious king, merciless champion and protector of the world, and claimed to have personally killed 450 lions.

He must have been a big cheese.

# Freaky Roman Emperor Facts

The Roman emperor Claudius made a law allowing people to fart at banquets. He was concerned about the health of people who were holding them in.

That farting law sounds sensible to me!

The Roman emperor Caligula had a favourite horse called Incitatus, who wore a collar made of precious stones and lived in a marble stable with an ivory trough.

The Roman emperor Commodus
enjoyed gladiator contests and
fought as a gladiator himself, but
he made sure he won by giving his
opponents weapons made of wood.

The Roman emperor Elagabalus
ate camels' heels, flamingos' brains
and cocks' combs, and he let wild
animals into his guests' bedrooms
while they were asleep.

# Freaky Fact

The Mayans and Aztecs chewed the resin from the sapodilla tree — an early form of chewing gum.

How did the Vikings communicate at sea?
**They used Norse Code.**

Which fruit started a war in
ancient Greece?
**Melon of Troy.**

What do you get in a posh pyramid?
**A tomb with a view.**

It would take me ages to tell you
everything about ancient Japanese
swords and weapons . . .
**But I could samuraise
it for you.**

# Frightful Fact

Wow!

Persian king Cambyses II
sent an army into the desert
to capture the Oasis of Amon.
The entire army of 50,000 men
disappeared in a sandstorm,
and people have been searching
for it ever since.

What do Stone Age people do on
a Saturday night?
**They go clubbing.**

Why did the Romans build
straight roads?
**So the Roman soldiers
didn't go round the bend.**

How do you ask to get into a
mummy's tomb?
**Toot-and-come-in.**

Did you know they used to hang signs
in ancient Egyptian funeral parlours?
**They said,
'Satisfaction guaranteed
or your mummy back'.**

# Funny Fact

The ancient Egyptians had a poetic name for the toilet: they called it 'the House of the Morning'.

What do you call a Roman Emperor who likes fresh fruit juice?
**Julius Squeezer.**

Slurp!

# Greek Monster Facts

The ancient Greeks had some of the best monster stories ever. They included:

snake-haired Medusa the Gorgon, who turned into stone anyone who looked at her;

the half-man, half-bull Minotaur, who lived in a labyrinth on Crete and feasted on sacrificial victims;

the Sphinx, with the body of a lion, the face of a woman and an eagle's wings, who strangled and ate anyone who couldn't answer her riddles;

Yikes! Not as scary as a cat though. . .

the half-woman, half-bird Harpies, who terrorised blind King Phineas by flying off with his food before he could eat it and pooing on any scraps that were left!

# Freaky Fact

In the 400s, near Aleppo in Syria, Saint Simeon Stylites lived on top of a pillar for 37 years. Other people followed his example, and holy men on pillars became quite common. Like Simeon, they were trying to live a life free from worldly pleasures.

Why are Egyptian mummies so stressed out? **They're bound to be uptight.**

Which Greek king invented
the fireplace?
**Alexander the Grate.**

Egyptian pharaohs were often
buried with a namafor.
*What's a namafor?*
**Knocking in nails.**

What do you get when you cross an
ancient Greek bull with a pig?
**A swine-otaur!**

How much is King Tut's
treasure worth?
**An arm and a leg.**

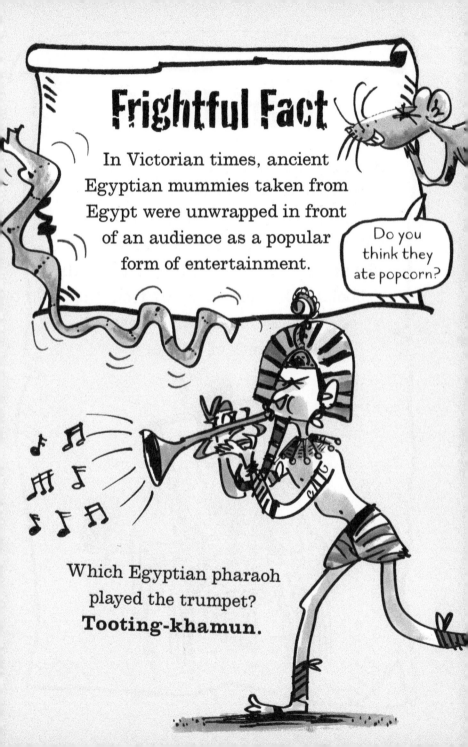

# Frightful Fact

In Victorian times, ancient Egyptian mummies taken from Egypt were unwrapped in front of an audience as a popular form of entertainment.

Do you think they ate popcorn?

Which Egyptian pharaoh played the trumpet?
**Tooting-khamun.**

# Fearful Fact

China's first emperor, Qin Shi Huang, is famous for his vast underground tomb filled with terracotta warriors. While he was still alive, he searched for an elixir of eternal life, ordered all books to be burned (apart from the ones in his library) and executed hundreds of scholars.

Knock, knock.
**Who's there?**
Sutton.
**Sutton Hoo?**

Who?

Why was Rome built at night?
**Because it wasn't built
in a day.**

What was a caveman's
favourite band?
**The Rolling Stones.**

Why didn't the Roman chicken
cross the road?
**Because she was afraid
someone would Caesar.**

# Funny Fact

The ancient Greek playwright
Aeschylus is said to have died
when an eagle dropped
a tortoise on his head.

What was the
most popular film
in ancient Greece?
**Troy Story.**

# Foul Fact

The ancient Romans used to bleach their hair with pigeon poo.

I thought bird poo was supposed to be lucky!

Ancient astronomers used to be up all night wondering where the sun had gone . . . **Then it dawned on them.**

What did the ancient Roman say
to his very loud friend?
**Be quiet. You're getting on
Minervas!**

Who was the famous religious
barbarian warrior?
**Attila the Nun.**

Why did the naughty ancient
Egyptian child get a detention?
**Because he let off
a Sphinx bomb.**

Why was Cleopatra always
saying 'no'?
**She was the Queen
of de-Nile.**

# Fascinating Fact

The ancient civilisations of the Indus
Valley had cities with roads, sewers
and toilets, but we don't know much
about them, and no one's been able
to decipher their language. But
we do know that the first dentists
practised there – drilled teeth have
been discovered there from
9,000 years ago.

Open wide!

You don't scare me!

# Fun Fact

The ancient Egyptians mummified animals as well as people, so that they could go on to the afterlife too. Mummified animals included cats, dogs, falcons, monkeys, gazelles, baboons, ibises and eels.

Did you hear about the
archaeologist who went
to the doctor?

**He was having problems
with his trowel movements.**

What do you give an Egyptian
mummy with a sore throat?
**Coffin drops.**

Why was the ancient Roman
hopping and shouting 'Ow!'?
**He'd stubbed his toe-ga.**

What did one pyramid
say to the other?
**How's your mummy?**

# Foul Fact

Ancient Greek doctor Hippocrates examined, sniffed and tasted his patients' earwax, sweat, snot and vomit.

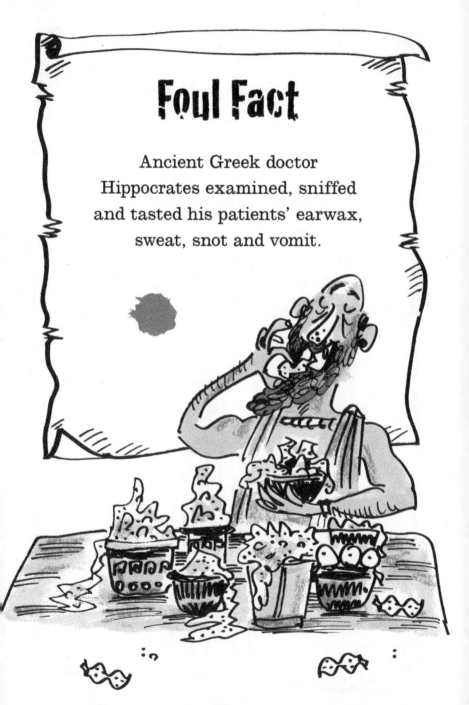

# Freaky Fact

Emperor Valerian ruled Rome from AD 253 to 260. He was captured by Shapur, leader of the Persians, and the story goes that he killed Valerian by making him eat molten gold, then put his straw-stuffed body on display in the Persian temple.

What did the ancient Egyptians
call camels without humps?
**Humphrey.**

Why did the Vikings sail to Britain?
**It was too far to swim.**

Time flies like an arrow.
**Fruit flies like a banana.**

Which ancient king had
the biggest crown?
**The one with the biggest head.**

Do mummies enjoy being mummies?
**Of corpse!**

What was the first thing King Aethelwulf
did when he came to the throne?
**He sat down.**

# Fascinating Fact

In just twelve years, Alexander the Great conquered an empire that stretched from the Mediterranean to the Himalayas. He died suddenly, aged only 32, after a huge party celebrating his victories.

Who was the fastest Aztec emperor?
**Monte-zoom-a.**

Look at him GO!

# Fearful Fact

Aztec punishments for children
included holding them in the smoke
of a fire made from burning chillies
and pricking them with
cactus spines.

Why did Queen Cleopatra
go to the dentist?
**To have her teeth crowned.**

Where are all kings and
queens crowned?
**On the head.**

What do you call the Greek monster
Medusa when she's asleep?
**A snorgon.**

What do you call a samurai warrior
armed with a long, sharp sword?
**Nothing. You just run!**

Why do history teachers make
rubbish cooks?
**Because they know more than
anyone about ancient grease.**

Smells like burnt sausages. . .

# Funny Fact

Xerxes I, emperor of Persia, gathered his army and navy ready to invade Greece, and made boat bridges across the Hellespont, a narrow stretch of the sea. When a storm destroyed the boat bridges, the story goes that Xerxes whipped the sea with chains to teach it a lesson.

# Frightful Fact

Cyrus the Great was defeated by a warrior queen, Tomyris of the Massagetae. The story goes that she used the dead king's skull as a drinking cup.

What's a mummy's favourite type of music?
**Wrap music.**

What does an ancient Greek
god wear to play sport?
**Tennis Zeus.**

Why did the ghost of Queen Elfrida
make friends with the demons?
**Because demons are a ghoul's
best friend.**

Why did Aztec emperor Montezuma
keep drawing straight lines?
**Because he was a ruler.**

Why can't you get Wi–Fi in the
Greek underworld?
**Because the Serverus down.**

# Fancy Fact

Today, diamonds are the most expensive precious stones, but the ancient Chinese didn't think much of them – they used them as cutting tools but not as jewellery.

Where do Egyptian mummies go swimming?
**The Dead Sea.**

A Roman soldier went to visit a friend and was amazed to find him playing chess with his horse. 'I don't believe it!' he exclaimed. 'That's the cleverest horse I've ever seen.'

'He's not that smart,' the other soldier replied. **'I've beaten him three games out of five.'**

# Fingernail Fact

Chinese scholars used
to grow their fingernails very
long to show they were too posh
and clever to do any manual work.
Some would have just one
super-long nail.

Smart idea –
I'm going to grow
a super nail too!

What do you call a vampire
Egyptian mummy?
**Wrapula.**

Squeak!

When were barbeques invented?
**During the Saus-Age.**

What's a good game to play with
a Greek monster?
**Hydra-and-seek.**

What do you call a rampaging
barbarian chicken?
**Attila the Hen.**

What did people use to write with
in ancient Peru?
**Inca pens.**

Where did ancient Greeks go
camping?
**A camphitheatre.**

# Fascinating Fact

People had forgotten how to read
Egyptian hieroglyphics but, after it
was discovered in 1799, a language
expert used the Rosetta Stone to
decipher them, because the stone
has the same words carved into it in
two different languages and three
different scripts.

What bounces along 5,000 miles
of northern China?
**The Great Ball of China.**

Which queen of the ancient Britons
was known as a bit of a cry-baby?
**Boo-hoodicca.**

QUEEN CLEOPATRA: Make ready a
bath of asses' milk – I wish to bathe!
SERVANT: Pasteurized?
QUEEN CLEOPATRA: Of course not.
**Just up to my neck.**

Anyone fancy a milkshake?

Where was Cicero beheaded
in ancient Rome?
**Just above the shoulders.**

# Fearful Fact

The samurai had elaborate, fearsome-looking armour and long, curved swords called *katanas*, and a variety of other weapons including metal fans for bashing people over the head. From the 1500s, they fought with firearms and cannons too.

Why are barbarian warriors always
tired on 1 April?
**Because they've just
completed a 31-day March.**

Cleopatra was considered
to be very beautiful.
**She was the pharaohs
of them all.**

# Frightful Fact

Julius Caesar was kidnapped by
pirates in the Mediterranean Sea,
who demanded a ransom for his
release. Once it was paid and Caesar
was free, he set off after them,
captured them and had the lot of
them executed, as he'd promised
when he'd been their prisoner.

# Fascinating Fact

The Aztecs and the Maya both wrote books made from tree bark, which folded like a concertina and were covered in jaguar skin. When they conquered South America, the Spanish burned most of the books.

Two people were whispering
about a statue of an ancient
Persian god . . .

**I think it was just idol gossip.**

Which huge Chinese construction
is made out of wool?
**The Great Shawl of China.**

Why did the ghost of Montezuma
never take sides?
**He was super-neutral.**

How many druids did it take to
change a light bulb?
**Twenty. One to change the
light bulb, the other nineteen
to realign the stones.**

# Foul Fact

The ancient Egyptians used the poo of pelicans, crocodiles, lizards and even people to cure a variety of illnesses.

What kind of art did cows make in ancient Rome?
**Moo-saic.**

That's the funniest joke I've ever herd!

# Flushing Fact

The first flushing toilets were flushed more than 4,000 years ago, in the Indus Valley and Minoan civilisations.

Which college did Montezuma go to?
**Az Tech.**

What do Suleiman the Magnificent
and Akbar the Great
have in common?
**The same middle name.**

How do mummies knock on doors?
**They wrap as hard as
they can.**

Why did Julius Caesar
cross the Rubicon?
**To get to the other side.**

The leaders of ancient
civilisations liked the sound of their
own voices . . .
**They did tend to Babylon.**

# Fearful Fact

The Anglo-Saxons had a system of payment if they injured or killed someone, depending on the injury and how important the person was. For example, killing a peasant cost 200 shillings, chopping off his nose cost 60 shillings and an ear cost 30.

# Fascinating Fact

Alexander the Great had a favourite war horse called Bucephalus. When the horse died, Alexander founded a city named Bucephala after him.

Why did Julius Caesar buy crayons?
**He wanted to Mark Antony.**

What happened when the ghost of
Montezuma got lost in the fog?
**He was mist.**

The Aztec snake god was called
Quetzalcoatl. But what was he called
when he tied himself in a knot?
**Pretzalcoatl**.

What do you call a sunken Viking
longship that shakes and shivers
on the seabed?
**A nervous wreck.**

# Fascinating Fact

Viking Leif Ericson sailed to North America around 1000 AD, nearly 500 years before Christopher Columbus's famous voyage. He landed on the island of Newfoundland, off the coast of Canada, and called it Vinland, but he only stayed for a year.

# Flood Fact

Aztec emperor Montezuma had seriously bad luck during his reign: there was famine, flooding, a plague of locusts and finally the worst luck of all – the conquering Spanish!

He must have been cheesed off.

Where do bunnies go on holiday?
**Easter Island.**

The Incas never invented
the wheel . . .
**It was Incan-ceivable
to them.**

What do you call a medieval monk
who likes making chips?
**A friar – he's also known as
the chip monk.**

What did the Roman say after
he made a mosaic?
**I am so tiled!**

What do you call an exact copy of
the Rosetta Stone?
**The Rosetta Clone.**

Where did the Incas get their
drinking water?
**From the Inca well.**

Nothing beats a bubble bath!

# Freaky Fact

When the Visigoths conquered Spain in the 400s, they destroyed the bath houses because they thought hot baths were too soft for tough warriors like them and might make them weak.

# Frightful Fact

The Aztecs practised human sacrifice
to appease their gods and they
sacrificed animals too. Jaguars,
dogs, deer and eagles were bred to
be sacrificed to the gods, and
butterflies and hummingbirds were
also sacrificed to the god Quetzalcoatl.

That was a narrow squeak!

What do history
teachers do when
they get together?
**They talk about
old times.**

What did Alexander the Grape
say when he was defeated?
**Nothing. He just let
out a little wine.**

Did you hear about the angry
Egyptian mummy?
**He flipped his lid.**

I want my
mummy!

At what time in history did people
have the neatest clothes?
**The Iron Age.**

What was the Forum in
ancient Rome?
**Two-um plus two-um**.

# Frightful Fact

In Vietnam in 40 AD, the Trung sisters led an army of 80,000 warriors, with 36 women generals among them. They drove the Chinese rulers out of Vietnam and became joint queens, but the Chinese came back and defeated them in the end.

What did ancient Greek children play with in preschool?
**Play-to.**

# Fascinating Fact

We have the ancient Babylonians to thank for the way we tell the time. The Babylonian number system was based on 60, not 10 like ours, and that's why we have 60 sections in a minute and 60 minutes in an hour.

What do you call the period when ancient Egyptians were making mummies? **The Band-Age.**

Why did it take two ancient
Greeks to carry a pot?
**Because they liked doing
things toga-ether.**

What's the difference between
the Iron Age and the Bronze Age?
**An I, a B, a Z and an E.**

How did people make friends in
the Stone Age?
**They joined clubs.**

Why didn't Socrates like chips?
**Because they were cooked
in ancient Greece.**

# Fearful Fact

Charlemagne, King of the Franks, conquered great chunks of Europe and founded an empire – the Holy Roman Empire – that would last nearly a thousand years. In his mission to convert everyone to Christianity, he executed 4,500 Saxons in one go.

What a rat!

Where do history books sleep?
**Under the covers.**

# Funny Fact

Aristotle, the ancient Greek
philosopher, taught his students
that insects have six legs.
Unfortunately, he also believed
that they generated spontaneously
from rotting meat.

Why did the Roman Colosseum
have to close?
**Because the lions had eaten
all the prophets.**

A Roman soldier lost his favourite sword in battle. A few weeks later, his horse walked up to him carrying the sword in its mouth. The soldier was amazed. 'It's a miracle!' he exclaimed as he took the sword. 'Not really,' said the horse. **'It has your name engraved on the hilt.'**

# Fascinating Fact

Many of our days of the week are named after Viking gods: Tuesday is named after Týr, the warrior god, Wednesday is named after Woden, the god of war and poetry, Thursday is named after Thor, god of thunder, and Friday is named after the Viking goddess of love, Freyja.

Who failed to unite the Mongolian
tribes and conquer a vast empire?
**Genghis Khan't.**

How do you tell if an ancient
Greek has a fever?
**Check his temple-ature.**

# Flute Fact

People have been playing music for
a very long time: a 35,000-year-old
flute was found in a cave in
Germany. It was made from
the bone of a vulture.

What's as big as a pyramid but
weighs nothing?
**Its shadow.**

Why was the mummy stressed out?
**Because someone had been
winding him up.**

What do you call an ancient Briton
who likes ballroom dancing?
**A Tango-Saxon.**

I prefer a cheesy cha cha myself!

Labels on bottles: Pelican poo. · Lizard poo. · Crocodile poo. · Person poo.

**TRACEY TURNER** writes for children about lots of different subjects, including rude words, deadly peril and the entire history of the universe. She studied classical civilisations at university, where she heard some truly ancient jokes – some of which are in this book.

**MARK BEECH** was studying fashion design when he realised he only really liked the drawing bit, so he changed career paths and has been inventing new characters and collaborating with many fantastic authors ever since. He has also built up a rather impressive collection of paintbrushes.